T16126

Introduction

Australia, which is officially named the Commonwealth of Australia, is known as the Land Down Under. The country lies in the Southern Hemisphere, so far south that it appears to be on the underside of the globe. Australia is one of the largest countries in the world, and it is the only country that is also a continent. Most Australians live on the southeast coast, where the land is fertile and plenty of rain falls. Few people live on the rugged, dry land in the center of the country.

Canberra is Australia's capital. It lies near the southeast coast, just south of Sydney. Most Australians speak English, but many of the Aborigines, people whose ancestors have lived in Australia for thousands of years, still speak their native languages.

3

Navy

The Australian flag has a **navy** background. The large seven-pointed Commonwealth star stands for the six states of Australia and the country's territories. The five stars on the right stand for the Southern Cross. This is the best-known constellation in the Southern Hemisphere, which is the half of the world where Australia is found.

In the upper left corner of the flag is a small Union Jack, the flag of Great Britain. This stands for the connection between Australia and Britain. Australia was once a group of British colonies. In 1901, Britain gave the colonies their independence, and they became one country, the Commonwealth of Australia. Britain's king or queen is still considered to be Australia's ruler, but this ruler has no real power in Australia. The country is independent.

6

Cream

Flocks of hundreds and hundreds of **cream**-colored sheep can be found in every one of Australia's states. Sheep were among the passengers on the first ship of European settlers, which arrived from Great Britain in 1788. By the early 1800s, Australians had discovered that their land, with its wide open spaces, was ideal for raising sheep. About the same time, the demand for wool was growing in Britain, so sheep ranching became an important industry for Australia. The growing wool industry brought many new settlers to the country.

The number of sheep in Australia has grown to more than 160 million. About three-fourths of the sheep are merinos, which are known for their high-quality wool. Australia produces more wool than any other country in the world.

Red

At the center of Australia is an enormous lump of sandstone, called Ayers Rock, that turns fiery **red** at sunrise and sunset. The red color comes from iron in the sandstone. Ayers Rock is actually the top of a buried mountain range. It's a six-mile hike around the rock, which rises more than a thousand feet above the surrounding plain. Ayers Rock lies in the Northern Territory, in a part of Australia called the Outback. The Outback is a wild area of deserts and rugged plains that makes up most of the country.

Ayers Rock is known as Uluru to the Aborigines, the first people of Australia. They consider the rock to be a spiritual place, and their ancestors have gathered there for perhaps the last ten thousand years. In 1985, the government of Australia gave the land on which the rock stands back to the Aborigines.

9

Gold

Cries of "**GOLD!**" rang out in Australia in 1851. That year, prospectors found gold in the colonies of New South Wales and Victoria. Thousands of people came to Australia with the hope of striking it rich.

The life of a miner was not easy. The work was hard and dirty, and water was scarce. Crime was common in gold-mining towns. If thieves didn't take a prospector's money, then the government would. Each miner had to pay a high fee, and there were heavy fines for those who didn't. Most people didn't get rich, but they decided to stay in Australia anyway. During the ten years the gold rush lasted, the population of Australia nearly tripled.

Aqua

British sea captain James Cook sailed his ship into the calm **aqua** waters of Australia's Botany Bay in April of 1770. At that time, the only people who knew much about Australia were the Aborigines, people who had lived there for thousands of years. A few other Europeans had landed in Australia, but Cook was the first European to explore the eastern shore. Captain Cook named his landing spot Botany Bay because of all the unusual plants his men found there. Botany is the study of plants. Cook claimed the eastern part of Australia for Great Britain and sailed for home.

Several years later, Australia's first European settlers set sail from England for Botany Bay. Most of these people were British prisoners being punished for minor crimes. They stopped for a short time at Botany Bay but soon found a better harbor a bit farther north. There the settlers founded Port Jackson, Australia's first European colony. Port Jackson was later renamed Sydney, and it became Australia's largest city.

White

The **white** roof of the Sydney Opera House looks like a ship's sails billowing in the wind. The beautiful building stands on Sydney Harbor in the Australian city of Sydney.

The design for the opera house was the result of a contest that brought in entries from architects all over the world. The winner was a Danish architect named Jorn Utzon. He thought the opera house would cost $7 million to build and would be finished in four years. Unbelievably, the building took nearly fifteen years to complete and the final cost was a whopping $102 million. Utzon grew frustrated during the long construction process and resigned seven years before completion. He never returned to see the finished building. The Sydney Opera House was officially opened in 1973 by Queen Elizabeth.

15

Green

Australia's most common tree is the eucalyptus, which usually has long, narrow leathery **green** leaves and is one of the world's tallest trees. Eucalyptus trees, which Australians call gum trees, can be as tall as a twenty-five-story building. They are found all over Australia, from the tropical regions on the coast to the deserts in the center of the continent.

Eucalyptus trees provide food for Australia's koalas. Koalas look like bears, but are actually related to kangaroos. A koala will eat more than two pounds of eucalyptus leaves every day. The leaves have so much oil in them that koalas can go for a long time without drinking water.

Yellow

The traditional paintings of Australia's Aborigines are often a rich golden **yellow.** The other colors used most often are red, black, and white. The paints are made from pipe clay, charcoal, and a mineral called ocher. Ancient Aboriginal art can be found throughout Australia on natural surfaces such as rocks and cave walls. Aboriginal artists also paint on large, flat pieces of bark. Aboriginal art often features human figures, animals like kangaroos, and many different shapes and patterns.

The Aborigines were Australia's first people. They lived there for thousands of years before the first Europeans arrived in 1788. The Europeans treated the Aborigines badly and took their land. By the 1800s, the Aborigines were in danger of dying out. Conditions for Aborigines have improved, but the people will probably never regain all that they lost. Painting in the style of their ancestors is just one of the ways they are trying to keep their traditions alive.

Gray

When you think of Australia, you probably picture a leaping **gray**-furred kangaroo. There are many different kinds of kangaroos in Australia, but the best known are the gray kangaroo and the red kangaroo. In spite of their name, many red kangaroos have gray fur. Both gray and red kangaroos have long, powerful back legs and short front legs. The animals can grow to be six feet tall and can weigh more than a hundred pounds. Kangaroos are marsupials, a group of animals that raise their newborn babies in a pouch on the front of the female's body. Other marsupials found in Australia are the koala, wombat, and Tasmanian devil.

Australia is one of the few places in the world where kangaroos roam wild. Besides Australia, kangaroos are only native to New Guinea and a few neighboring islands. The kangaroo is such an important symbol of Australia that it appears on everything from the country's coat of arms to many of its coins and stamps.

Coral

Many of the corals that make up Australia's Great Barrier Reef are **coral** in color. The reef is also many other colors, including yellow, purple, green, and blue. A coral reef is a wall of coral that ends at the surface of the water. Coral reefs are formed by tiny creatures called polyps. When polyps die, they leave behind their outer skeletons, which we call coral. Other polyps attach to these skeletons. When they die, their skeletons add to the reef. That's how a coral reef grows.

The Great Barrier Reef is the world's largest coral reef. It is actually a region of over 2,500 individual reefs that stretch for more than 1,200 miles off the northeastern coast of Australia. The reef is home to about 1,500 different species of fish. Other creatures living there include sponges, starfish, crabs, sharks, turtles, and giant clams.

23

Index

Aborigines, 3, 8, 12, 18
Ayers Rock, 8

Botany Bay, 12-13

Canberra, 3
Capital, 3
Cook, James, 12
Coral, 22

Eucalyptus trees (gum trees), 17

Flag, 5

Gold rush, 11
Great Barrier Reef, 22
Great Britain, 5, 7, 12-13, 14

Kangaroos, 17, 18, 21
Koalas, 17, 21

Land, 3, 7, 8, 17
Language, 3
Location, 3

Name, official, 3, 5

New South Wales, 11
Northern Territory, 8

Outback, 8

Port Jackson, 13

Queen Elizabeth, 14

Settlers, European, 7, 11, 13, 18
Sheep, 7
Size, 3
Sydney, 13, 14
Sydney Opera House, 14

Tasmanian devil, 21

Uluru, 8
Utzon, Jorn, 14

Victoria, 11

Wombat, 21
Wool, 7

For Evan and Alex, with my unending love—LOA

To my mom, who urged me toward children's books—JLP

Map on page 3 by John Erste

Text and illustrations copyright © 1997 by Carolrhoda Books, Inc.

This book is available in two editions:
Library binding by Carolrhoda Books, Inc.
Soft cover by First Avenue Editions
c/o The Lerner Publishing Group
241 First Avenue North
Minneapolis, Minnesota 55401 U.S.A.

Library of Congress Cataloging-in-Publication Data

Olawsky, Lynn Ainsworth.
  Colors of Australia / by Lynn Ainsworth Olawsky ; illustrations by
Janice Lee Porter.
      p.   cm. – (Colors of the world)
  Includes index.
  Summary: Uses colors to focus on the history, physical features,
and culture of Australia.
  ISBN 0-87614-884-4 (lib. bdg.)
  ISBN 1-57505-213-X (pbk.)
  1. Australia—Juvenile literature. 2. Colors, Words for—Juvenile
literature. 3. Color—Juvenile literature. [1. Australia.
2. Color.] I. Porter, Janice Lee, ill. II. Title. III. Series.
DU96.045 1997
919.4—dc21   96-45651

Manufactured in the United States of America
1 2 3 4 5 6 – SP – 02 01 00 99 98 97

994

Colors of
AUSTRALIA

by Lynn Ainsworth Olawsky
illustrations by Janice Lee Porter

𝄞 Carolrhoda Books, Inc. / Minneapolis